# CASCADING THOUGHTS

NATASHA SHARMA

*This book is dedicated to my mom. You might have never had a budding interest in poetry but you have always motivated me to write whatever I felt like. You are my role model, who has held my hand through the highs and the lows.*

# Contents


*Preface* — vii

*Prologue* — ix

*About The Author* — xi

1. Expression — 1

**Nature And Hope**

2. Mesmerized — 7

3. Nature's Fury — 9

4. The Tale Of The Wind — 10

5. Delight — 12

6. Moonlight — 13

7. Wolves — 15

8. Change — 16

9. Those Days — 18

10. Tommorow — 19

**Life**

11. Digitalized — 23

12. Dream? — 24

13. Love — 26

14. Modern Chaos — 28

15. Somebody — 29

16. Introspection — 30

17. Introversion — 31

18. She — 33

19. New Life — 34

# Contents


20. I Am — 36

21. Insecurities — 37

22. Friendship — 39

23. Loved — 41

24. Reminder — 42

25. Bliss — 43

26. An Ode — 45

27. Butterflies? — 46

28. Fantasy? — 47

**Breaking Free**

29. A Girl — 51

30. Equality? — 53

31. Judgement — 54

32. It Is Okay — 55

33. Chapter 33 — 57

The Very End ;) — 59

# Preface

Looking through the diary of poems I have written in since I was 13, I realised in the past 4 and a half years, I have evolved like every normal human being would but what I also realised is I have emotions that are utterly conflicting. I never really believed in sitting down and looking into nothingness to write a piece of poetry, I write what I see and what I think is right. And apparently my definition of what is right keeps changing!!

That got me to thinking, "What if I am really not the only one whose emotions dictate what she writes, whose thoughts wander so much that what she percieves to be right one day seems the complete opposite the next time she sits to write!" And Lo and behold! This book full of all my poems came into being. I sincerely hope that you like what I write!

~ Natasha :)

# Prologue

**Cascading Thoughts**- a book that is all about the things that make me, well me. A random yet quite organised set of poems and paragraphs I wrote since pretty long. The name of the book is basically how I have always written down my thoughts, I always wrote strings of words and tried to make sense of them later when that fountain of thoughts ended and I always ended up with a poem or a paragraph in hand. It was a long process even to compile just about 33 chapters in this book, because believe me writing a book is NOT an easy task.

Enough about me, I hope you enjoy the randomness of my poems and at the risk of sounding presumptuous appreciate the work put in. XD

# About The Author

*NATASHA SHARMA*

*Natasha is a student with a head full of conflicting thoughts, an ever-ready smile on her face, and a pen in hand at the ready-to-scribble. Crusty old pages are addictive for her and if you ever wish to find her, the first place to look would be a quiet corner with a book in hand. Poems are an outlet of emotions for her, written words are the best way she knows how to express them. She hopes this book is a good read for you!*

# 1. Expression

*When I write,*
*It is a temporary refugee, a blissful respite.*
*An act of breaking free,*
*From my mind ghastly errors unsee.*
*It is like a flow, a flow of thoughts I can never spell out, not one*
*string*
*holding me back now, this expressive freedom makes my heart*
*sing.*
*No chaotic mess, no striving for finesse,*
*It is just me, my words, my thoughts, and no unrest.*
*A garland of words, making me feel they know me the best.*
*A blanket of comfort if you may, it is almost absurd,*
*for these are words that were always left unheard.*
*Writing is a solace,*
*a trusted accomplice, in the crimes of writing the truth.*
*The sketch of words I draw, making a poem the fruit.*
*It is a peek into my soul, a way to unwind and narrate the*
*untold.*
*It plays many a role.*
*Poems are words untainted,*
*raw, my feelings since forever they painted.*
*Making me scribble on,*

*not once leading to a frown.*
*But some poems I slid into the unknown,*
*the emotions wrapped were too real to be shown.*
*~Natasha*

*Poetry always taught me to be real, to be true to what I feel, to nurture emotions and imaginations but still stay connected to reality. This poem is like a tribute, a tribute to the memories of me scribbling down words and connecting the dots to turn it into something that held meaning. A tribute, to the many times it gave me a chance to pen down what I never could have spelled out loud. A tribute to the times when poems turned my giggles and my teardrops into words that yearn to be heard.*

*IT IS A TRIBUTE TO THE POWER OF EXPRESSION.*

NATASHA SHARMA

# Nature and Hope

I hold my love for nature very dear, but it has led to many a conflict in my mind as well. The poems that follow will take you through my journey of appreciation and my fear of nature as I went on observing and discovering.

Hope, that might just be my favorite word. Honestly, as human beings, we have the power to be positive and we should use it in the best possible way. Hope keeps us going and after all that we have faced, it is a necessity to hope for a better future.

# 2. Mesmerized

*I stood quietly, gazing at the dusk, its ethereal beauty,*
*It captivated me enough to make me forget each duty.*
*It made me crave a hug, not from a person but the nature's hug,*
*a beautiful, mesmerizing feeling that I would never shrug.*
*Away from the cacophony of just being,*
*the peace was so freeing.*
*The charisma of the crimson sky,*
*assured me nothing would go awry.*
*Liberated, an escape from fear and worry,*
*for once made me feel I am not living my life in a hurry.*
*A sense of tranquility, it gave me no purpose but to live.*
*Nature and its mesmerzing beauty, solitude they do give.*
*The serene summer breeze, ending a day,*
*welcoming the night, the only time when humans have no say.*
*The beauty gives rise to a mirage*
*an illusion, but a hauntingly beautiful spark.*
*Shimmery sky, stars, a speck in the vastness of the night*
*The heart gives in to the mesmersing allure without a fight.*
*Leaving me with no memories that haunt*
*a smile on the face, when happiness seems so scant.*
*I walk away atlast,*
*for moments like these go away just as fast.*

# CASCADING THOUGHTS

*Nature might daunt,*
*but never does it flaunt*
*of its power*
*Only endless beauty it blesses us with, as a shower.*
*~Natasha*

# 3. Nature's Fury

*It started with a welcoming breeze,*

*an invitation to the day seize.*

*The swift rustle, caressing each leaf*

*making the bees buzz, and a smile on our faces keep.*

*It felt like a breathing being,*

*Gentle and beautiful, but was it really all that we were seeing?*

*It was full of beauty unlike any,*

*a gift of much-needed peace to many!*

*But it started to pick up speed,*

*moving around a lot faster that what we need.*

*And then it turned wild,*

*scaring each child.*

*Nature is beautiful no doubt, but it still is utterly scary,*

*if it rages, humankind must stay wary.*

*It is responsible for love and laughter,*

*but still makes us want to hold on to our lives much tighter.*

*The amazement of its beauty may leave us numb,*

*but to its wrath many have had to succumb.*

*~Natasha*

# 4. The tale of the wind

*Smile, why don't you!*
*Look how the wind just blew, right past you.*
*Whispering into your ears,*
*the secrets, it has heard through all these years.*
*I wonder if it remembers, the ashes and those embers*
*from the bonfire we had in December!*
*How ethereal the wind is, eternal*
*It has heard the wails on each dead man's funeral.*
*And heard the joyful cries when each baby was born,*
*it has suffered through the torture of listening to each car's*
*incessant horn.*
*It is ever-present like a gentle caress,*
*What love and warmth it does possess.*
*Sometimes it picks up pace, whistling,*
*brings with itself some wistful drizzling.*
*But sometimes it is angry and strong,*
*almost as if nature is punishing us for all we have done wrong.*
*Enjoy the respite of the wind while it lasts,*
*don't keep dwelling on your pasts.*
*Listen to it, whisper past*
*for some, it might as well be the last.*
*Let the wind help you unwind,*

*from the hustle of being alive, take off your mind.*
*– Natasha*

# 5. Delight

*The clouds in the sky spoke of better dusk the next day,*
*A sunlight morning, with a hint of intrigue,*
*left with nothing to say.*
*They brought the sun and the wind to speed.*
*A moonlit night sky, with a blanket, stitched with each intricate*
*star,*
*The couple lay on a blanket of their own and looked from afar.*
*The moon heard of their ideal date,*
*told the stars to put a stopper on their fate.*
*Give them one night to remember,*
*A romantic night in the cold beauty of December.*
*The moon and the stars whispered amongst themselves, "Let's give*
*them a beautiful existence,*
*Even if to ruin themselves, they are so very persistent."*
*~ Natasha*

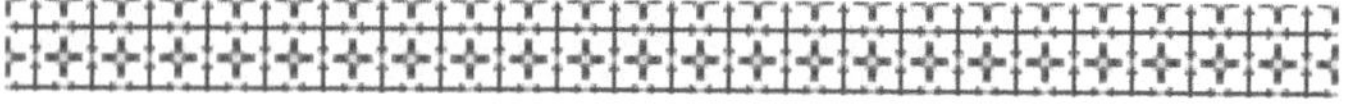

# 6. Moonlight

*The moon glistened bright,*
*shedding light, all night.*
*It rose above the lake,*
*the water turned silver in its wake.*
*All creatures had retired,*
*even the fish were now tired,*
*but no matter what the moon kept shining.*
*It gave a couple the perfect night for dining,*
*it gave a poet the reason to put pen to paper.*
*It silently gave respite to a teenager's thoughts that society didn't*
*shape her.*
*The moon gave the wolves a reason to call out,*
*sometimes even made fain-hearted, in the dark, shout.*
*It was the perfect background to the creaking of trees,*
*and rustling of leaves through the steady night-time breeze.*
*The moon accompanied the stilness of night,*
*reminding the birds to go back home, as they took flight.*
*The moon was haunting and beautiful,*
*giving moments of amazement and serenity, bountiful.*
*In silence too hear the moon's story,*
*you might even forget all that you have to worry.*
*It has so much to say,*

*you will want to stay.*
*~ Natasha*

# 7. Wolves

*The moon gives peace in moments.*
*The wolves keep howling in the distance.*
*They almost seem to warn us of the nights,*
*the end of days that hide within themselves*
*the intrigue of better or worse.*
*The wolves are alone but a pack almost as if human.*
*Aren't we all alone in crowded rooms today?*
*The power they hold in each snarl through the dark side of the*
*moon,*
*is like a call to the gods of the wilderness.*
*We say we are humans but within ourselves we hold an intrigue.*
*When they said we are all wolves howling to the same moon,*
*it didn't make sense until it just did.*
*~Natasha*

# 8. Change

*Looking out of the window,*
*the roads are deserted.*
*Well, humankind maybe you have by isolating yourselves,*
*you have from yourselves grave danger averted.*
*No cars, no pollution, no humans to deforest*
*Everything happens to lead to something good.*
*Millions have died, true*
*But look at how the world has changed, why don't you?*
*When we get out of this we will know to self-introspect,*
*how the environment has changed in our absence, reflect.*
*The deaths, always will stay with us, make us tear up*
*but it will be a reminder of how we didn't give up.*
*Someday when we will look back, there always will remain a*
*silver lining,*
*of how we reconnected to our roots, let the environment*
*rejuvenate.*
*One day when we sit down and remember this time, we will*
*realise how useless*
*it is for us to cry of the lack of luxuries in life*
*When the whole world was fighting and the nature provided us*
*respite,*
*yet we were ignorant enough to always keep it under a knife.*

NATASHA SHARMA

*~ Natasha*

# 9. Those Days

*I agree we are all scared, we fear not knowing what we are*
*facing.*
*Thinking how is it an endless facade we are chasing?*
*Locked up in our houses, nowhere left to go.*
*Life seems to almost standstill, with no change, so very slow.*
*Then hits the realization, is this what a caged animal feels?*
*How are we so helpless? Is this how it feels when,*
*to circumstances, our will kneels.*
*Yet, we all see how we are all making the best of our time*
*in what seems like an endless quarantine.*
*It has been difficult no doubt, but all those we hold dear are*
*together.*
*Relations, long-estranged seem a lot better.*
*Our fear for the worst has brought us closer,*
*the hostile lines drawn, we had between us seem to blur.*
*- Natasha*

# 10. Tommorow

*So it happens to be a new day,*

*or that is what anyone would say.*

*It is supposed to be happy, they say*

*not meaning to be sappy.*

*We are stuck in our homes,*

*Last Christmas was at home, surrounded by gnomes.*

*It seems to be endless,*

*the virus on its killing spree, it is relentless.*

*Another new year is around the corner,*

*A new beginning for each mourner.*

*Maybe it will be a better year,*

*isn't that all we hear?*

*But truly hoping is the only thing we can do,*

*It is easier said than done, true.*

*But this year too, pleasure in the small things we found.*

*That is all that kept us healthy and sound.*

*The optimist within us is fighting to smile.*

*The pessimist wants us to worry, go senile.*

*It's up to us to work our way through.*

*Find happiness, even if those moments are far and few.*

*Let this be a lesson, to never underestimate nature,*

*not even its littlest creature.*

*For even one mistake, can the world from its root shake.*

*~ Natasha*

# Life

*There are some things that we notice in our day-to-day lives, some might be good some not so much! This section is all about such observations that I make daily and tend to write about.*

*HAPPY READING!*

# 11. Digitalized

*It's a generation of smiling faces with a broken heart,*
*the amount of pretense, no idea where to even start.*
*It is all about pretty posts hiding the ugly truth,*
*the only way is to be "IT", productivity being the only thing*
*laying fruit.*
*It is chaos, but we all try not to make a fuss,*
*yet we are all living our lives in such a rush.*
*Laughing out loud is just LOL in a text,*
*not the real deal.*
*Stop! Think! These days do we even remember how to feel?*
*Apparently, we are whiling away our lives, ruining our future.*
*We are waiting for that, "You are a disappointment ", the*
*lecture.*
*A pocket full of dreams, and eyes shining bright we still live on.*
*For in this fast gen-z not even sadness is ever set in ston*

# 12. Dream?

*Some days, you look back and the moments you see seem like they were just a dream or maybe at times nightmares! It is like life passed by so quick that we forgot how to live, we drifted past the moments that mattered and now all we have left are memories! And these memories are so blurred and distant that they snuggle you in a blanket of comfort but still possess an undertone of unrealism.*

*These dreams are beautiful nonetheless, they revisit us when we need them the most and hold the pieces ready to break together until we heal and let them go. The problem with moments in our lives is that they aren't all good, so sometimes our dreams are just nightmares that should never have returned. And these moments we wished to forget rush back in, leaving us in a mess. Your heart feels like it's stuck in your throat and you can't gulp it down. But then again, no one claimed life is always easy. Maybe, we all are living in a dream. Maybe, we all are just a result of someone's beautiful yet scarring imagination. But the point is, we all are here. In this present moment, I am writing this. And over the course of days or months, you would be holding this in your hands and reading this looking out the window at the cold winter sun, or you might be wrapped in a blanket burrito hiding this book or any other behind your school books, pretending to study. No matter what, we are all living and breathing and I think that is beautiful, and we should enjoy it. Let us not let any of these moments we have in our lives become blurry figments of our imaginations.*

*Dreams are beautiful, but let us all live those dreams before making them a distant memory to relive years later. Stop! Prioritize living life, not rushing through it, one day you might not have these people you love by your side, and if you don't stop and enjoy them, no memories left of them either. Let this be your dream that you never wake up from.*

*- Natasha*

# 13. Love

*Doe-eyed, rosy-cheeked, I remember that child in me,*
*She loved, she hoped and she was free.*
*Today it is a generation of fast-moving attraction,*
*Loving only until it reaches your satisfaction.*
*And I am a victim of the same,*
*But honestly, I don't say this in shame.*
*I say this when I remember the girl who believed in love so true,*
*She wished each night for the one who would hold her hand and*
*say. "No matter what I am always with you",*
*But now she knows, people leave, memories stay.*
*No matter how many times you wish they would disappear in a*
*day.*
*I remember the girl who believed in the fantasy of "the one",*
*Of the world conspiring to make me meet him and make me feel*
*like I have won.*
*I miss that girl who giggled with her friend,*
*about that one guy, who they gave a nickname so no one gets a*
*hint.*
*That girl had so many dreams of eternal love*
*How his hand would fit her's like a glove.*
*And that girl, she was adorable.*
*But I guess time changed love for her, made it horrible.*

*But somewhere inside her heart she still wishes on a shooting
star,
"Just give me one hint who he is, I promise I will look only from
afar."
This generation has changed us all,
It uncool, in love, to fall
We have started to hate empathy,
in this society with no sympathy.
We think we are asking for too much,
each time failing and breaking our hearts, just a touch.
But I guess that dreamy teenager in me, she doesn't care
She still believes, in love all is fair.
~Natasha*

# 14. Modern chaos

*It's all about that craze,*
*that one-sided daze.*
*That waiting for a special embrace,*
*waiting to look at that one person's face.*
*It is about being patient,*
*being tested, staying complacent.*
*Listening to the whispers of this chaos,*
*not being able to be together just because.*
*It is about fighting your own will,*
*having to sit still.*
*Not knowing what to do but hope,*
*that even today in all this, your future together has a scope.*
*It is about staying positive when*
*the future seems bleak.*
*And there seems to be nothing,*
*left in life to keep.*
*- Natasha*

# 15. Somebody

*Doesn't everyone need a shoulder to cry on,*
*a someone with a bond set in stone.*
*Doesn't every person need a reliable smile,*
*when you are down, to hold you up for a while.*
*Each person needs a hand to hold,*
*to give back your love tenfold.*
*Doesn't every person need a friend or maybe someone more,*
*To bring you back to the shore.*
*To help throw away each worry,*
*promise to hold your hand through thick and thin firmly.*
*That somebody is there, we all deserve one,*
*who we can look to after each battle we have won.*
*~ Natasha*

# 16. Introspection

*Do you ever actually ask the one in front of you,*
*"Are you okay?", or do you just believe the pretense to be true?*
*Do you ever make an effort to make someone smile?*
*Sit down, talk just give them company for a while?*
*Maybe not others, but do you even ask yourself, "Am I able to*
*cope?",*
*Do you sit down and think, "I am positive, there still is hope!"?*
*If you haven't, it isn't too late! Go spread some love and joy!*
*Remind all those out there,*
*no other human is worthy of being played with like a toy.*
*Remind yourself, relations keep you going in life,*
*They give you the strength to never lose hope and take up a knife.*
*Be the reason for laughter yours and others,*
*it may sound a little too ideal,*
*But making even one person smile,*
*it will make your day worth living*
*for real!*
*- Natasha*

# 17. Introversion

*I have not one ounce of shame when they say, "You are so*
*introverted!",*
*because truly I am a better "me" when left deserted.*
*Alone, that is how I learned the ropes,*
*knew how to keep up with their hopes.*
*For me, I was a ship that I helped maneuver,*
*But people around say, "Her heart is colder than a night in*
*Vancouver!"*
*You see that has been me since I was knee-high,*
*questioning myself about the blue, blue sky!*
*Fast-forward to the present, nothing much has changed,*
*my introversion is still very famed.*
*In my heart, I remain the same,*
*my thoughts are different, I have grown older, I don't have the*
*same mind frame.*
*Being an introvert has been uselessly demonized,*
*shown to the world as something to be despised!*
*An introvert is as much a human,*
*as any other outgoing man or woman.*
*Your personality is for you to develop and decide,*
*not for others to dissect, it is for you to take pride!*
*Being shy and quiet in social situations is not always a curse,*

*Just remember it could have been a lot worse!*
*~Natasha*

# 18. She

*She stayed awake at night,*
*Her sleep she would fight.*
*She was caught in the hurricane of her unsmiling past,*
*She knew she ought to move away from it, fast.*
*She was like a rose, but her thorns pricked more.*
*It made people forget the beauty of each petal.*
*She couldn't keep on proving her mettle,*
*She lived in self-doubt and in her mind questions,*
*against her own worth arose.*
*But she decided to change who she was.*
*Live with a meaning, stop making a fuss.*
*Realization struck, how all depended on her,*
*if she preserves or throws away, her future.*
*The roset hat she was,*
*was in full bloom.*
*Away from the place which,*
*reeked of gloom.*
*- Natasha*

# 19. New Life

*The changing level of mediocrity,*
*A fast moving city.*
*The link to reality is a mess,*
*people are being played like it is a game of chess.*
*What in the world is this chaos!*
*In my ears, I can hear the sound of loss.*
*Living our lives with avarice,*
*and we call this glamourous!*
*Walking on a path with no way back,*
*today we live in the world where noone can cut any slack.*
*Wishing upon a shooting star,*
*maybe it can save us from afar?*
*I wonder if we can wander,*
*away from this place, I know it is very easy to ponder.*
*Wishing to live a life full of boundary less thrill,*
*We have forgotten the beauty of unadorned living, the peace in*
*sitting still.*
*Maybe this is just a way of coping,*
*a different way of hoping.*
*Life is full of speculation,*
*no way to get ou of constant contemplation.*
*-Natasha*

# 20. I am

*I am, sounds so incomplete, doesn't it? But do you ever stop and think? If you would, you would understand how it is the most sensible and complete statement. You are whatever you wish to be, beautiful, ambitious, caring, indecisive, apathetic it may be good for you and not for those who wish to be different but if for you, you are happy with your "I am", it will make sense every time. Who cares if your hair isn't the best in town! Who cares if you think your teeth are too crooked, smile. Who cares if you have a little belly fat! who cares if you love putting on makeup or you don't, who cares if you can't live without dressing up or you can't get out of your pyjamas. And if anyone cares or judges, don't spare them a thought, you are great the way you are until you don't get lost in your own head. For you, "I am what I choose to be, not what that boy or girl in my class said I should be", you aren't what others wish for you to be or what the society says is "perfect". You are you.*

*You just are, you aren't someone's idea of you.*

# 21. Insecurities

*It was old yet new,*

*for everyone around me I seemed happy, maybe so did you.*

*But, did you ever notice how me and you we laughed a little too hard?*

*Did it not occur to those other people, that the happiness we projected might be a farce?*

*In a way, we were hiding the hurt? and it had become a daily charade?*

*People assume everyone else's lives are perfect,*

*don't realise maybe in this assuming world, they might not have anything worth it?*

*Passing smiles, laughing like all jokes mean so much, maybe that is pulling them apart..*

*No one knows what is happening around,*

*In our own lives we are too bound.*

*We self-depreciate, even when in ourselves there is so much to appreciate*

*Because all we are to ourselves are people who are trying to be perfect*

*for everyone in their lives become worth it.*

*Maybe we know we all are anything but,*

*and when we let our mind stray it starts closing upon us.*

*Maybe that is why we have become a generation of people*
*with emotions shut,*
*People call us heartless, we don't correct them*
*They could be right.*
*On these assumptions, we have stopped picking a fight.*
*But this is a sign for you, you are worthy-enough.*
*You have stuck to being you, even when it gets tough.*
*You have breathed through it all, the lack of give and take.*
*Your emotions, atleast them you shouldn't fake.*
*Don't pull yourselves down, don't let them fill your mind with*
*insecurities and doubts,*
*those are all untrue.*
*You are enough, be happy and don't let them get to you.*

*~Natasha*

# 22. Friendship

*Friends are truly for life, and I realised this in the past few months, after my school life ended. I was anxious that over the course of time I would end up losing all of my friends that I had for so many years of my life always there supporting me, fighting with me, loving me or sometimes even hating me. But what I realised when the time came was that I didn't make these friends I earned them and I earned their love, loyalty and even dislike at times for life. Distance wasn't what decided if we all were friends, it was the true bond we shared that defined the course of our friendship. So I sat down to write a letter to all my friends who I earned and lost in these years.*

*Dear people who I might or might not be in contact with,*

*This one is for you all, those who still believe that I deserve their friendship and those who might not even remember my name anymore. In these years, days, or months that we haven't met every day and shared moments with each other I realised how far along all of us have come from the first time we met. I still remember how religiously we celebrated Friendship days and birthdays, with chocolates and who gets to go out. Still makes me laugh how even fights have ensued in this selection. Those good old days when we were all so naive. Today when I look back, I realised how you all made life better just by existing. Each of you has a special place in my heart and even if we don't talk anymore you will always be remembered fondly.*

*We all had our ups and downs as friends, we might not have ended our friendship the best way, but I hope I gave you enough good memories to last a lifetime and forgive me for the worst. We might not talk to each other anymore but your memories still mean the world. Maybe we might not need each other right now, but thank you for standing by my side when I did. Maybe I am not the reason for your smile today, but I promise when you need a dose of laughter you can count on my horrible sense of humor any day.*

*You all have taught me some lessons that I will never unlearn, you have given me memories to cherish for a lifetime, you have given me laughter and smiles when my world felt bland. So thank you to you all for choosing to be my friend and creating memories with me.*

*May this open letter find you happy as ever, with a beautiful smile gracing your faces, at your best. We all are off to new places and ready for new experiences but I will always remember all of you for the butterflies in my tummy, the toothy smiles and the endless laughter.*

*With love,*

*Natasha*

# 23. Loved

*To all those people I used to love and do not talk to anymore,*
*You all have pieces of my heart, grasping them unknowingly in*
*your fist*
*Honestly, I find it okay to let the piece be, for once you were the*
*reason for my smile, my happiness in a gist.*
*Don't worry, I am not asking for my shard of heart back, it can*
*survive with you*
*I promise, I gave it away willingly because all I wanted was to*
*start anew.*
*And that little part of my unshattered heart, you it can never*
*hate*
*Even if the memories of "us", they fade.*
*I am no longer, the naive girl who ignored each sign*
*My thoughts, they have aged like fine wine.*
*I hope, like me, you too have filled your heart, those empty spaces*
*With renewed passion loved, new and unfamiliar faces.*
*Yes, I did love you but of forever too early I spoke,*
*I am alright with it, because finally we are out of the ignorant*
*smoke.*

*Natasha*

# 24. Reminder

*People told me, love means butterflies in the stomach,*
*giving yet taking too much.*
*But when I thought of love, It reminded me of peace,*
*it reminded me of the buzzing bees, the flowers which blossom*
*the sunlit windows in London.*
*it reminded me of the smell of the pages of a new book,*
*of the beauty in a downpour, of a stranded boat finding a shore.*
*Love for me, meant something enchanting*
*slow yet daring, leaving you weak in the knees*
*but holding your hand, into the night staring.*
*Love gave me reasons to rule out insecurities,*
*making me feel like I was a work of art.*
*Love for me is like poetry.*
*Love is a reminder of everything beautiful, right from the start.*
*Natasha*

# 25. Bliss

*When the sun had set and beyond,*
*When the moon had shone for hours already*
*The time when the bees had stopped buzzing*
*The time when even crickets are done chirping.*
*This was the time when the inhibitions she held slipped out of*
*her hands*
*into the night sky they ran.*
*When she was alone, but not lonely.*
*When the only sound heard on the empty paths*
*were the crackle of leaves beneath her feet*
*and the murmur of the breeze rustling her hair.*
*Her thoughts took flight in the dark of the night,*
*when the only illumination of her fears were her own thoughts.*
*She looked up at the moon,*
*it was nothing special yet it offered her the familiarity of home.*
*Walking back, she breathed in the last of her night time bliss,*
*bid adieu for the night to the warm breeze and the yellowing*
*leaves.*
*Waiting for the next night, bringing the promise of*
*another few minutes of blissful respite.*
*Natasha*

# 26. An ode

*When it is time to write of me, write from the start.*

*Write of how once, I would do each thing with my heart.*

*Write about those thoughts I had, no one was around,*

*How with breathtaking silence, loved to myself surround.*

*Write of broken hearts, and battles I wish were better fought.*

*Write of how I put love and consideration in each thought.*

*Don't just show how everything changed,*

*show them how all the people I wished to be, I became.*

*Write of my love for books and tiny quotes,*

*how I wrote random strings of words in my notes.*

*Write about my love for poetry, all but a doe-eyed dream.*

*Of my love for stars, strawberry and cream.*

*Write of my battle with fears, all the wiped tears*

*Of smiles passed to every passer-by,*

*Of how i would look lovingly at the sky.*

*Write, I want to remember it all.*

*the love-struck me or how in love, I could never easily fall.*

*When I watch it again from heaven or hell, my life feels like a*

*movie, I would love to recall.*

*-Natasha*

# 27. Butterflies?

*There is peace when you are around,*

*a different kind of happiness you surround.*

*A love, I imagined I would never live,*

*You have given me more than I could ever give.*

*I see you smile, and I smile broad.*

*These days, to more mornings I look forward.*

*Imagine a day with you, makes me feel a certain way,*

*You can give me those non-fluttering just stable butterflies with a*

*simple, "HEY!".*

*It is a good kind of scary to love someone like you,*

*The kind of slow rush, ironic and felt by a few.*

*No fast heartbeats, just a loving gaze,*

*In my life, you are like a cool breeze on summer days.*

*~ Natasha*

# 28. Fantasy?

*We talked, The moon and I*
*We talked of the beauty of the stars*
*We talked about the truth behind our scars*
*We murmured to ourselves, of things so true*
*I told the moon of me and you.*
*Charmed into believing that forever existed,*
*a head full of thoughts and a head in the clouds.*
*I took to the stars, told them how I find them*
*How they are more than mere spots in the sky*
*Told them how they are the bacdrop of the fantasy of You and I.*
*I told all but you, of the words I yearned to say*
*I just kept them aside and walk away.*
*I am happy, you never knew*
*of the beautiful image I had of me and you.*
*~Natasha*

# Breaking Free

*I have always hated stereotypes, so I write to make people aware of how oppressing these stereotypes can become! Being put into moulds is not how we should live, we all have the right to be free, free from judgment and free from the shackles of roving eyes and ready mouths.*

# 29. A girl

*There is a girl, she is free,*
*her dreams are big and that is all she wishes to be.*
*She doesn't wish for fate's wonderful kiss,*
*She doesn't believe in chances of a hit and miss.*
*That girl, she is always gaurded, she protects her heart*
*She fears that if she let go, all would fall apart*
*She cherishes herself, never really asks for help.*
*But there always are others who ruin a story,*
*make it a tad to gory.*
*Harsh words, judgments passed,*
*in secret in her reflection she cries.*
*Why is it always about tearing up reputation?*
*What is with this ruthless fixation?*
*That girl, she feared rejection*
*she feared the consequences of her imperfection.*
*But she was blessed with friends and family alike, who let her*
*look past dejection.*
*Made her gloss over other's disaffection.*
*This girl I talk about, she is within all of us,*
*waiting and biding her time to rise up from the dust.*
*This girl, fixes up her dainty heart, and she does as she wishes,*
*beggining*

*right from the very start.*
*Natasha*

# 30. Equality?

*When we say equality, what do we mean?*
*Certainly not what is currently on our T.V. screen.*
*When we say equality, we mean equal rights.*
*For empowerment we lead these fights.*
*When we say, men and women are at par,*
*We mean they should all respect each other, not tear each other*
*apart.*
*When we fight for women empowerment,*
*we fight for equal respect and acceptance, its attainment.*
*Not for overpowering either of the two,*
*but those who truly understand happen only to be a few.*
*Each human, no matter the gender*
*faces the same society, remember?*
*Respect a human,*
*not their being a man or a woman.*
*Each person is fighting their own battle, may it be behind a*
*closed door.*
*One word of appreciation, may bring them happiness to their*
*core.*

Natasha

# 31. Judgement

*They keep saying, "Stick to one person, will you!?"*
*But what they fail to notice is that it wasn't her feelings that*
*were untrue.*
*They keep judging her for others' mistakes.*
*She remains silent, even though her heart breaks.*
*They didn't count how many times, her heart was broken.*
*Just looked at numbers, and thought her character was forsaken.*
*Enough.*
*You don't get to judge her after hearing one side of the story!*
*Paint a picture so gory!*
*Have you ever cared enough to hear the tale behind her tears,*
*The many betrayals over the years?*
*You can pass judgements all you want,*
*Being fair and listening, that you can't.*
*You talk of her behind her back, make fun of each tear,*
*but when you are with her, you are the sweetest I swear.*
*Ironic, you aren't what you show.*
*Well, one day you will reap what you sow.*
*~Natasha*

# 32. It is okay

*The edge of darkness,*
*no matter the finesse.*
*Every word trapped inside of her,*
*When she is alone, they come out in a spur.*
*Acted as if all was peachy,*
*inside her mind, anxiety was screeching.*
*When someone did break the walls and asked,*
*if she were alright, her feelings she always masked.*
*They asked, "What is it? Why do you seem so sad?"*
*"Is there a reason or have you simply gone mad?"*
*They don't understand, anxiety never needs a reason*
*to your body, at any time it can commit treason.*
*No one ever talks about mental health,*
*it is all about the hustle and the wealth.*
*And then they ask, why did you put on a mask?*
*Telling us, was that such a diffucult task?*
*Even if, you passed no judgement, which is rare,*
*in this world, all is unfair.*
*If she smiles, she is ecstatic,*
*if she rolls her eyes, how rude and sarcastic.*
*In this facade, no one looks at how nights for her, alone with the*
*feelings*

*were colder than a cold night in the arctic.*
*Honestly, there needs to be a discussion.*
*Or no one would be able to handle the repercussion.*
*In times like the present, everyone needs support and due*
*guidance.*
*Natasha*

# Chapter33

*Does anyone really know what they are doing? Not just the ever-popular Gen-Z, I mean everyone. We all are just grasping at straws and hoping that we are going on the right path. But still, we are forced to "decide" what we want to do when we are little kids, extremely annoying right? How is a five-year old supposed to answer the teacher when she asks," What is your ambition?", as a kid we just spit out the pre-fed, hard-wired answer in our little brains, "I want to be a doctor, an engineer or a pilot or a lawyer", because yes these are the only respected answers you can give.*

*Growing older, uncles and aunties at gatherings ask you with such high hopes, "Aage ka kya socha hai?" and God forbid you are in a "board" class, you will have to answer the incessant questions about which stream you wish to take and honestly the only acceptable answer is science with maths. And ofcourse the repeated questions regarding our chosen proffesions.*

*This whole rant was only to tell you, it is okay to not have it all figured out or have no answers at all, and it is also okay to know exactly what to do with your life. Do not feel like it is something you should feel inferior about or doubt yourself because. You have a long life ahead of you to make these decisions, there is no need to feel pressured into making such life-altering decisions beacuse some adults think it is okay to expect a 16 or 18 year old to plan out their lives when theirs is not even close to what they expected.*

# The Very End ;)

The book is not much of a read, it is a start. There are poems and paragraphs in this book at random just like my thoughts. It is just an embodiment of all the thoughts that have come to my mind over the years of my writing. Writing a book is a difficult task and honestly it is almost three months later that I have finished it with a mere 30 chapters to read. But before this gets self-depreciating, I will just thank you all for reading this random collection of writings put together by a completely naive human.

GOOD LUCK <3